my itty-bitty bio

Bruce Lee

Published in the United States of America by Cherry Lake Publishing Group
Ann Arbor, Michigan
www.cherrylakepublishing.com

Reading Adviser: Beth Walker Gambro, MS, Ed., Reading Consultant, Yorkville, IL
Book Designer: Jennifer Wahi
Illustrator: Jeff Bane

Photo Credits: page 5: © 4045/Shutterstock; page 7: TAMYAMMIA SHA/Wikimedia Commons; page 9: © xian-photos/Shutterstock; pages 11, 22: © Olga L Galkina/Shutterstock; page 13: © New Africa/Shutterstock; pages 15, 23: © Rawpixel.com/Shutterstock; page 17: © neftali/Shutterstock; page 19: © Mary Evans/STUDIOCANAL FILMS LTD/Alamy Stock Photo; page 21: © Lifestyle Travel Photo/Shutterstock

Copyright © 2023 by Cherry Lake Publishing Group
All rights reserved. No part of this book may be reproduced or utilized in any form or by any means without written permission from the publisher.

Cherry Lake Press is an imprint of Cherry Lake Publishing Group.

Library of Congress Cataloging-in-Publication Data

Names: Loh-Hagan, Virginia, author. | Bane, Jeff, illustrator.
Title: Bruce Lee / by Virginia Loh-Hagan ; illustrated by Jeff Bane.
Description: Ann Arbor, Michigan : Cherry Lake Publishing, 2023. | Series: My itty-bitty bio | Audience: Grades K-1 | Summary: "This biography for early readers examines the life of Bruce Lee, an icon in martial arts cinema, in a simple, age-appropriate way that helps young readers develop word recognition and reading skills. Includes table of contents, author biography, timeline, glossary, index, and other informative backmatter. The My Itty-Bitty Bio series celebrates diversity, covering women and men from a range of backgrounds and professions including immigrants and individuals with disabilities"-- Provided by publisher.
Identifiers: LCCN 2022043045 | ISBN 9781668920152 (paperback) | ISBN 9781668919132 (hardcover) | ISBN 9781668921487 (ebook) | ISBN 9781668922811 (pdf)
Subjects: LCSH: Lee, Bruce, 1940-1973--Juvenile literature. | Actors--United States--Biography--Juvenile literature. | Martial artists--United States--Biography--Juvenile literature. | Martial artists
Classification: LCC PN2287.L2897 | DDC 791.4302/8/092 [B]--dc23/eng/20220909
LC record available at https://lccn.loc.gov/2022043045

Printed in the United States of America
Corporate Graphics

2

table of contents

My Story 4

Timeline 22

Glossary 24

Index 24

About the author: When not writing, Dr. Virginia Loh-Hagan serves as the Director of the Asian Pacific Islander Desi American (APIDA) Center at San Diego State University. She identifies as Chinese American and is committed to amplifying APIDA communities. She lives in San Diego with her very tall husband and very naughty dogs.

About the illustrator: Jeff Bane and his two business partners own a studio along the American River in Folsom, California, home of the 1849 Gold Rush. When Jeff's not sketching or illustrating for clients, he's either swimming or kayaking in the river to relax.

my story

I was born in 1940 in California. Later we moved to Hong Kong. I grew up with two sisters and two brothers.

How big is your family?

My father was a **performer**. My first movie was with him. I was 9 years old.

I learned **martial arts** at 13 years old. I studied **kung fu** with Yip Man. He was one of the greatest teachers.

I also **competed**.
I moved to the United States.
I was 18 years old. I taught kung fu.

What do you like to do?

I made my own style. I mixed kung fu, boxing, and **fencing**. I started a school.

I fell in love and got married. My wife was White. **Mixed-race** marriages were illegal in many states then. We had two children.

I moved back to Hong Kong.
My family moved with me.
I became a big movie star.

We returned to the United States.
I became the greatest movie fighter.
I starred in *Enter the Dragon*.

I died in 1973. But my legacy lives on. I made kung fu popular.

What would you like to ask me?

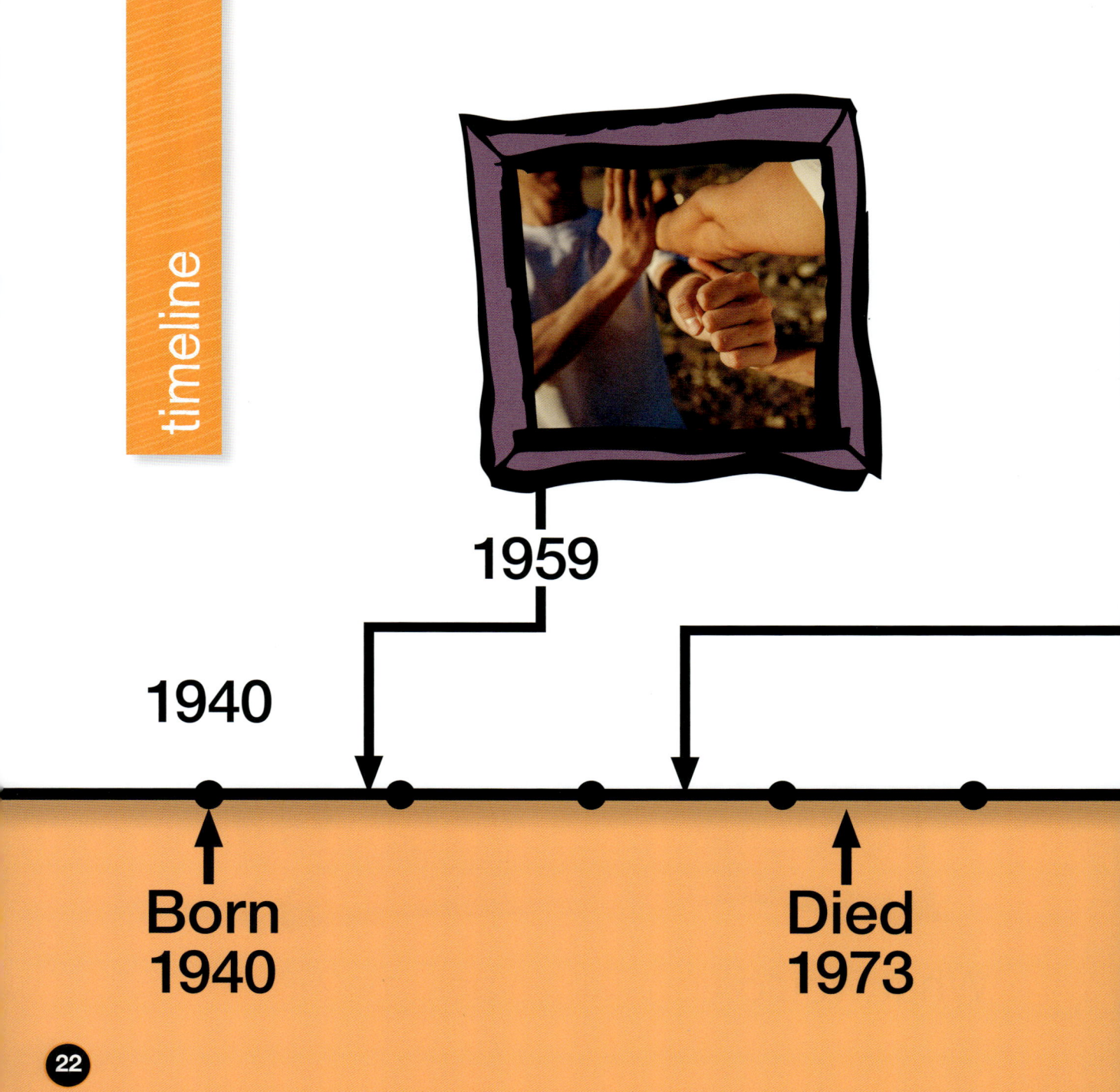

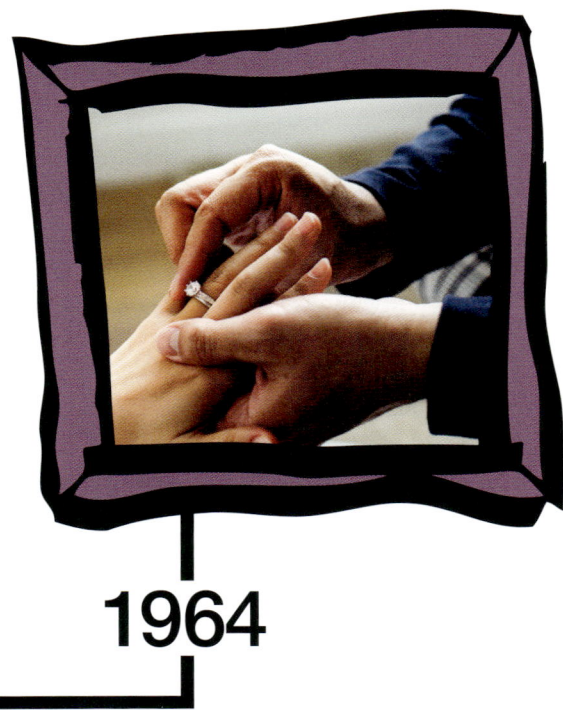

1964

2040

glossary & index

glossary

competed (kuhm-PEET-ehd) tried hard to outdo another person in a contest for a prize

fencing (FEN-sing) the art or sport in which a saber is used for defense and attack

kung fu (KUHNG FOO) an ancient Chinese method of self-defense by striking blows using fluid movements of the hands and legs; also known as gung fu

martial arts (MAR-shuhl ARTZ) forms of combat and self-defense that are widely practiced as sports

mixed-race (MIKST-RAYS) relationship between people of different races

performer (puhr-FOR-muhr) a person who acts, dances, or sings in front of others

index

birth, 4, 22

California, 4

death, 20, 22

Enter the Dragon, 18–19

family, 4–7, 14–15

Hong Kong, 4–5, 16

kung fu, 8–13, 18, 20–21

marriage, 14–15

martial arts, 8–13, 18, 20–21

movies, 6, 16–19

teaching, 8–10, 12–13

timeline, 22–23

Yip Man, 8